ALTERNATOR
BOOKS™

INSIDE
THE BERMUDA
TRIANGLE

TOP SECRET

MEGAN HARDER

Lerner Publications ◆ Minneapolis

For my family

Lerner Publications Company
An imprint of Lerner Publishing Group, Inc.
241 First Avenue North
Minneapolis, MN 55401 USA

For reading levels and more information, look up this title at www.lernerbooks.com.

Main body text set in Aptifer Sans LT Pro.
Typeface provided by Linotype AG.

Editor: Lauren Foley **Designer:** Athena Currier **Photo Editor:** Annie Zheng
Lerner team: Sue Marquis

Library of Congress Cataloging-in-Publication Data

Names: Harder, Megan, author.
Title: Inside the Bermuda Triangle / Megan Harder.
Description: Minneapolis : Lerner Publications, [2023] | Series: Top Secret (Alternator Books) | Includes bibliographical references and index. | Audience: Ages 8–12 years | Audience: Grades 4–6 | Summary: "Disappearances and other strange phenomena in the Bermuda Triangle have long inspired speculation and theories. Theorists chalk it up to everything from bad weather to time warps. Explore the mysterious history of the Bermuda Triangle"— Provided by publisher.
Identifiers: LCCN 2022015332 (print) | LCCN 2022015333 (ebook) | ISBN 9781728476629 (Library Binding) | ISBN 9781728478340 (Paperback) | ISBN 9781728485423 (eBook)
Subjects: LCSH: Bermuda Triangle—Juvenile literature.
Classification: LCC G558 .H37 2023 (print) | LCC G558 (ebook) | DDC 001.94—dc23/eng20220718

LC record available at https://lccn.loc.gov/2022015332
LC ebook record available at https://lccn.loc.gov/2022015333

Manufactured in the United States of America
1-52243-50683-7/5/2022

TABLE OF CONTENTS

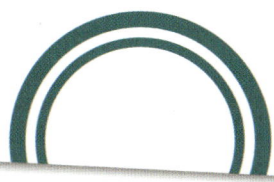

Form No. I
THIS CASE ORIGINATED AT

REPORT MADE AT	DATE WHEN MADE	PERIOD FOR WHICH MADE	REPORT MADE BY
	8/2/I9 : 9/2/I9		67c
	I/28/20 : 3/I2/2I,4/0I/22		67c
TITLE	I /5/22,	CHARACTER CASE	
		SECURITY MATTER – C	

THE DISAPPEARANCE OF *CYCLOPS*

Cyclops **was on a critical mission.** This *Cyclops* wasn't the one-eyed monster of Greek myths. The USS *Cyclops* was a collier, a special ship made to transport coal that could refuel other ships at sea. In March 1918, *Cyclops* carried something more precious: 12,096 tons (10,973 t) of manganese ore. The metal is an important ingredient of steel. It would be used to make the weapons American soldiers needed during the ongoing World War I (1914–1918).

But *Cyclops* never made it to her destination in Baltimore, Maryland. After stopping for supplies at the Caribbean island of Barbados, the ship was never heard from again. It was as though the boat and the hundreds of people on board had been swallowed whole!

Did *Cyclops* have a structural problem? Was she sunk by an enemy submarine? Or was her mysterious disappearance related to the area she vanished in—the infamous Bermuda Triangle?

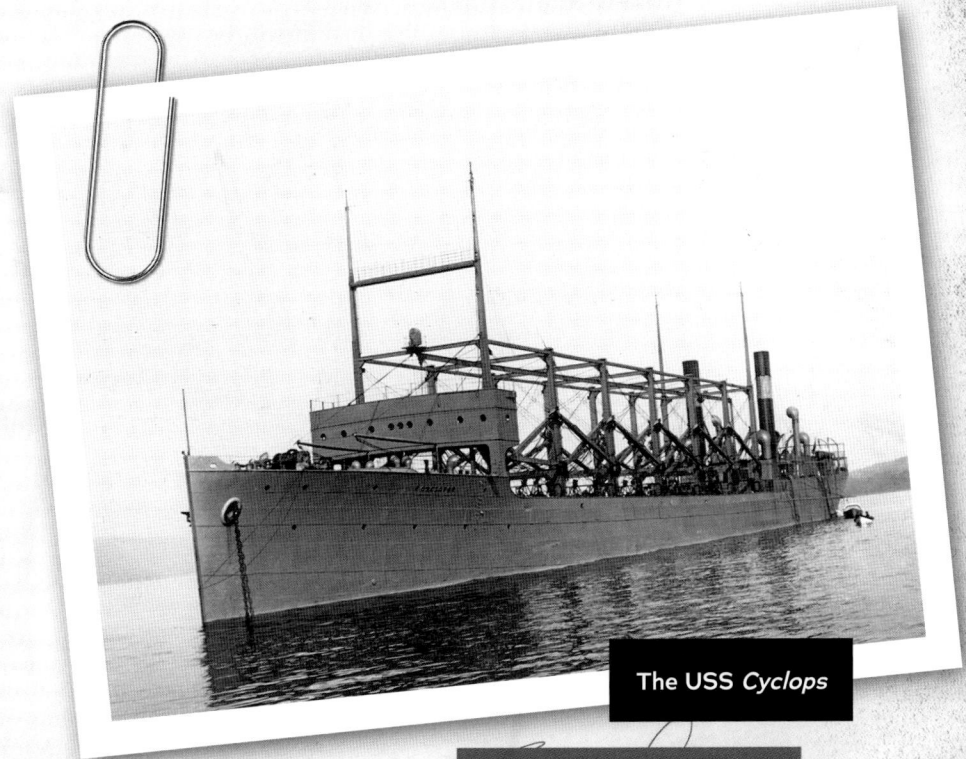

The USS *Cyclops*

CHAPTER I
A MYSTERY IS MAPPED

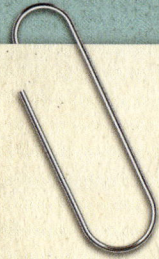

Storm clouds over the sea near Florida

This map shows the Bermuda Triangle's corners at Bermuda, Florida, and Puerto Rico.

You won't find the Bermuda Triangle on any official maps. The imaginary boundary contains about 500,000 square miles (1.3 million sq. km) of ocean and islands. Its corners align with Florida, Puerto Rico, and Bermuda. Although the area wasn't yet named the Bermuda Triangle in 1918, *Cyclops*'s mysterious disappearance wasn't the first strange thing to happen there.

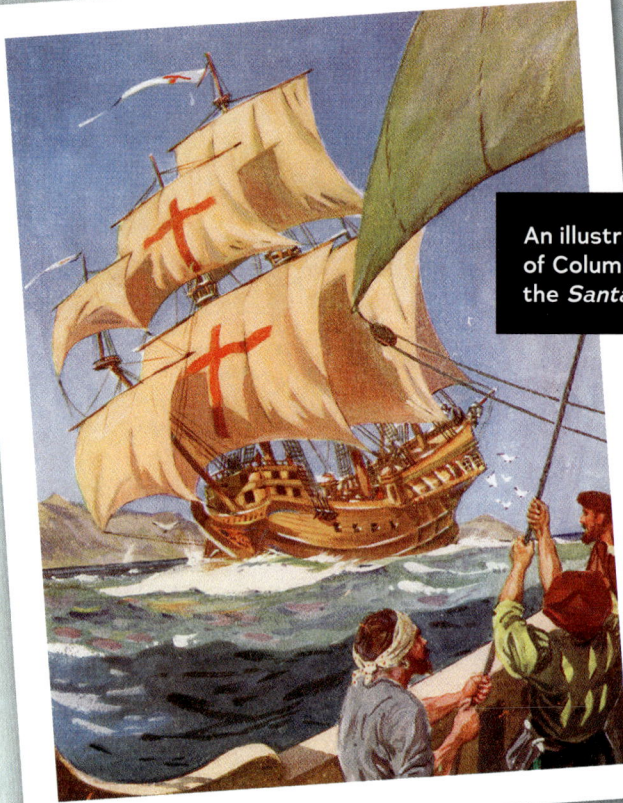

An illustration of one of Columbus's ships, the *Santa María*

Strangeness at Sea

Strange events have been reported in the Bermuda Triangle since the 1400s. During Christopher Columbus's first voyage across the Atlantic in 1492, he and his crew witnessed three unusual things. First, they saw a fireball fall from the sky. A few days later, the compass pointed off course. The night before the ships found land, some of the men witnessed a strange light hovering above the sea. Was it a sign of people nearby, or was it something more mysterious?

Columbus may have seen unexplainable things in the Bermuda Triangle, but his ship did not vanish there. Yet since then, the region has been blamed for the mysterious disappearances of dozens of ships. The *Patriot* vanished after setting sail in 1812 while carrying former vice president Aaron Burr's daughter to New York. *Cyclops*'s sister ship, the USS *Nereus*, disappeared in the triangle in 1941. Even vessels thought to be unsinkable, like the *Witchcraft* in 1967, have vanished there.

Some ships that traveled through the Bermuda Triangle have been found abandoned. People called them ghost ships.

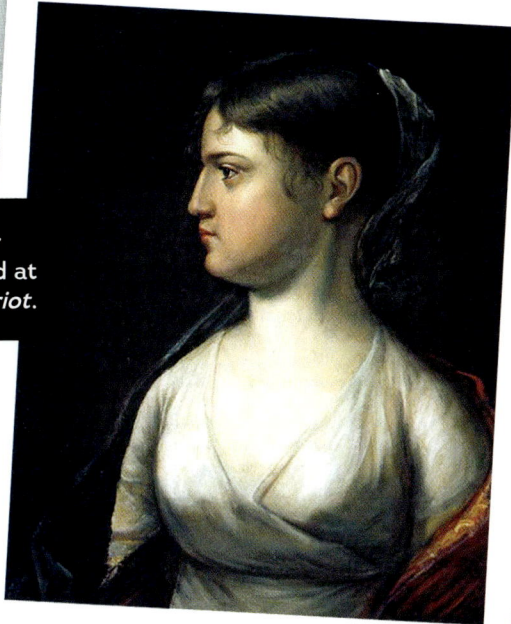

Theodosia Burr Alston vanished at sea on the *Patriot*.

One of these, the *Carroll A. Deering*, washed up near the North Carolina shore in 1921. Some even say its table was still set for dinner! Did something or some*one* make them disappear?

Flights to Nowhere

The odd disappearances didn't stop with ships. Many aircraft have mysteriously disappeared over the region. But none top the disappearance of six planes in one day. What should have been an easy training flight on December 5, 1945, became a tragedy when a group of five TBM Avenger torpedo bombers called Flight 19 got lost

Flight 19 was made up of a group of Avenger bombers like these. The planes have never been found.

Many planes are thought to have vanished or crashed in the Bermuda Triangle.

off the coast of Florida. Then one of the seaplanes sent to locate survivors disappeared too. No wreckage was recovered from these planes.

Flight 19 captured people's attention. They began to wonder why so many ships and planes had vanished without leaving clues behind. In the 1950s, writers began reporting the pattern they saw emerging. This zone of mysterious disappearances was given many names like Limbo of the Lost and the Devil's Triangle. A 1964 magazine article first called the region by its shape. The Bermuda Triangle was born.

CHAPTER 2

EXPLAINING THE UNEXPLAINABLE

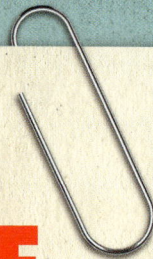

Dense fog can make it hard for plane and ship navigators to see.

A towering wave rising from the sea

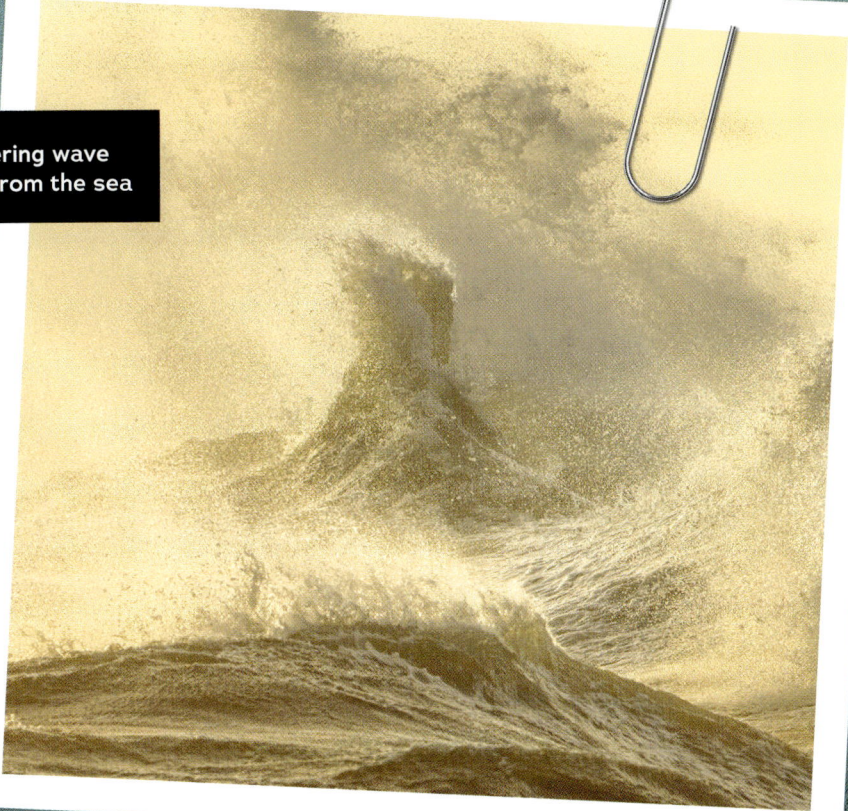

What do aliens, rogue waves, and the lost city of Atlantis have in common? All have been blamed for the Bermuda Triangle disappearances! While vanishing airplanes and ghost ships are mysterious, some of the theories about them sound unbelievable.

Some people think aliens in UFOs, or unidentified flying objects, snatch planes, ships, and people from the Bermuda Triangle.

Strange Theories

One popular theory suggests that aliens abducted the ships, planes, and passengers. Believers in this theory claim that extraterrestrials collect humans to study us or to monitor our technology.

Another idea is that an electromagnetic anomaly was disrupting space and time within the triangle, causing victims to enter another dimension. Electromagnetic anomalies could explain reports of compasses and communications equipment not working in the area.

Some people claim that the mythical island of Atlantis causes the electromagnetic changes. Although there is little evidence to suggest that Atlantis ever existed, believers say that an area of large rocks jutting from the seafloor near the Bahamas is the ruins of the sunken city. They argue that these ruins hide advanced technology once used to produce energy and power aircraft. This ancient technology is even thought to give off energy that interferes with planes and ships traveling through the Bermuda Triangle!

Supporters of these theories say that too many have vanished without a trace to be a coincidence. They argue that these disappearances are impossible to explain by natural causes. But others disagree.

This illustration shows what Atlantis might look like, assuming it existed.

SOLVE IT

////////////////////////////////

The Bimini Road is a long, underwater stretch of rocks in the Bermuda Triangle near the Bahamas. Some people claim that the Bimini Road is left over from Atlantis. Others say that it's natural rock that has cracked in a way that looks like human-made pavement. What evidence might support the idea that people built it? How could you prove that it is a natural formation?

The Bimini Road

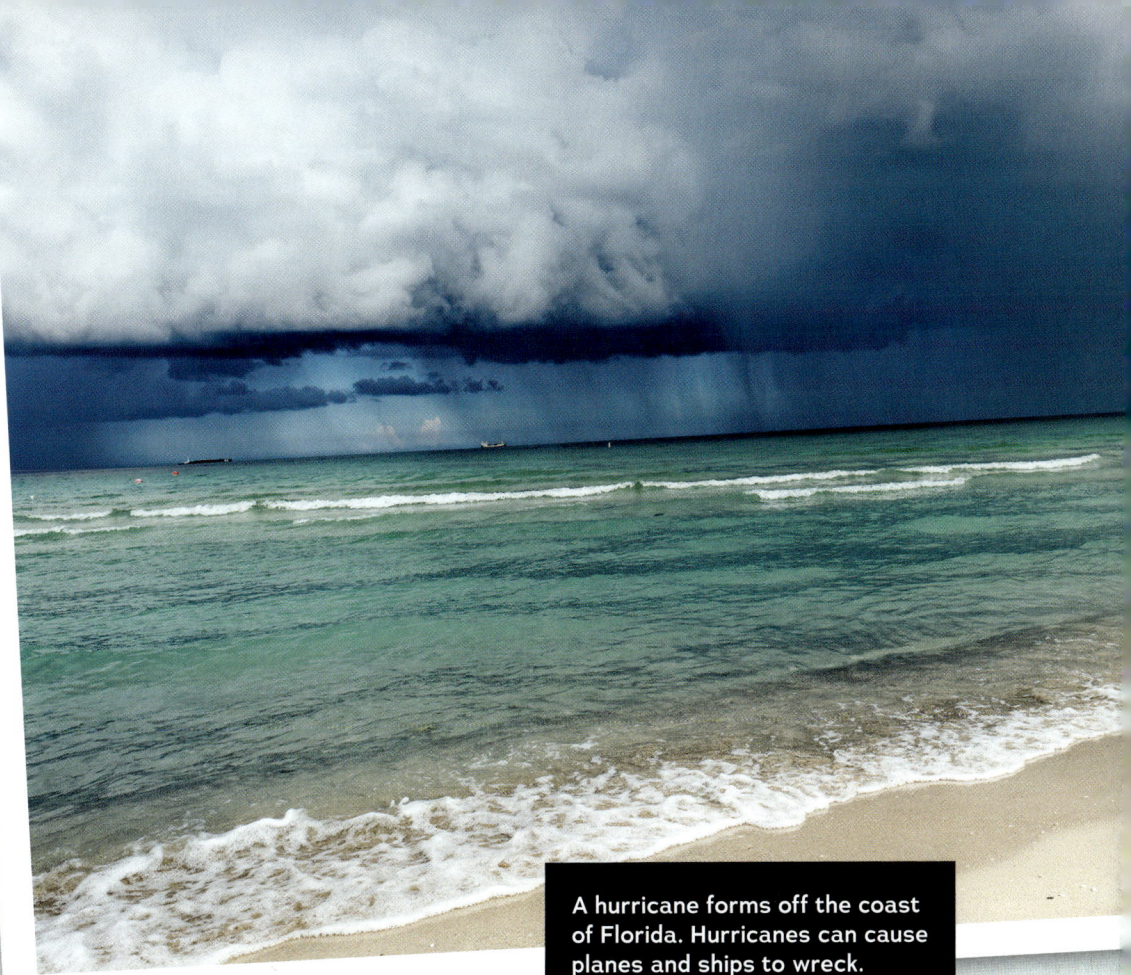

A hurricane forms off the coast of Florida. Hurricanes can cause planes and ships to wreck.

Natural Explanations

The Bermuda Triangle is home to many known dangers. From the 1500s until the 1800s, pirates prowled the waters, ready to strike ships carrying valuable goods from the Americas. Reefs and sandbars in the shallow waters around islands can snag ships, leaving them stranded or wrecked. In summer and fall, deadly hurricanes lash the Atlantic with fierce winds and heavy rain.

Waterspouts can destroy planes and ships at sea.

Unusual natural phenomena that can rapidly sink a ship or down a plane also exist in this area. Tornadoes that form at or move to the sea, called waterspouts, can destroy ships and planes in their paths. Towering waves sometimes appear in otherwise calm seas. These rogue waves can reach heights over 95 feet (29 m).

People can also cause disasters at sea. Mistakes like making a wrong turn or running out of fuel can be deadly when far from land. Badly designed ships might sink quickly in a storm.

SOLVE IT

Late on January 29, 1948, the *Star Tiger* was due to land in Bermuda after the world's longest overseas commercial flight. Strong wind slowed down the plane. The aircraft was still far away an hour after it was supposed to land. The *Star Tiger* was never seen again. Did it run out of fuel? Could it have flown off course? What's your theory?

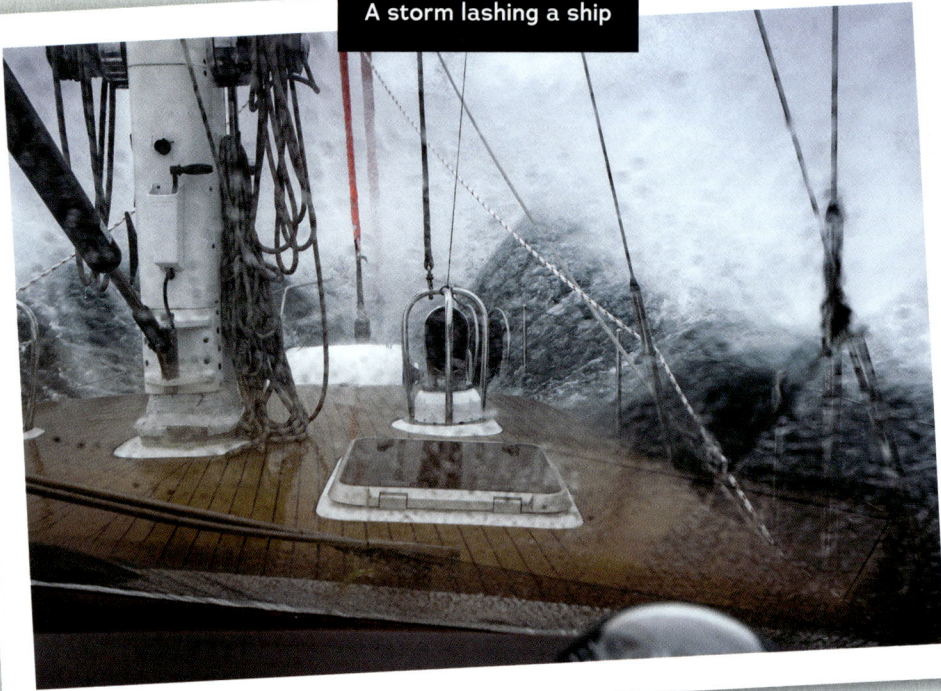

A storm lashing a ship

Between human error and natural disaster, many things can go wrong. Most likely one or more problems caused disasters for each disappeared ship or plane in the Bermuda Triangle. The loss of Flight 19 could have been the result of a navigational error and running out of fuel in bad weather. Perhaps pirates sunk the *Patriot*. Or maybe she was lost in a storm. Without survivors, witnesses, or proof, we can only guess what happened to the ships, planes, and people lost in the Bermuda Triangle.

A navigator helps decide a ship's course. Even with modern technology, sometimes navigators and other crew members make mistakes.

CHAPTER 3

THE TRIANGLE'S DEEP SECRETS

A shipwreck at the bottom of the sea

Rescuers use helicopters and other technology in their searches.

Even as safety measures and technology improve, it's still tough to find aircraft and ships lost at sea. Unlike on land where a plane will stay where it crashes, planes and ships wrecked at sea may settle deep below the surface. Currents can also move debris. Rescuers focus their searches where they think they will be successful. But if they have inaccurate information, search parties might look miles away from the missing vessel.

On March 8, 2014, far from the Bermuda Triangle, Malaysia Airlines flight 370 (MH370) disappeared over the Indian Ocean. An international search cost millions of dollars. But it failed to locate the lost jet. It took sixteen months for debris from the plane to appear. It showed up on beaches thousands of miles from MH370's last known location. When Flight 19 disappeared in 1945 or the *Patriot* was lost two centuries ago, no one likely thought to look for debris a year later and 2,000 miles (3,218 km) away.

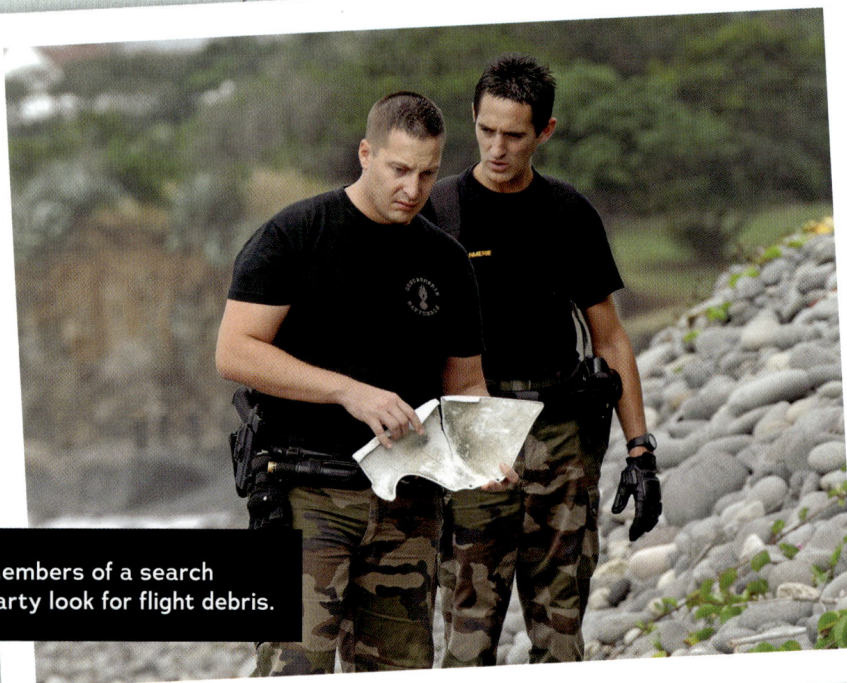

Members of a search party look for flight debris.

The SS *Cotopaxi*

The story of MH370 shows the challenges of finding a ship or plane that has been lost at sea. Even known wrecks can be hard to identify after years of breaking down underwater. This happened to the SS *Cotopaxi*, a collier that went missing in the Bermuda Triangle in 1925. Some people claim that the *Cotopaxi* was yet another victim of mysterious forces. No one knew what became of the ship until 2020, when it was proven that a shipwreck found in the 1980s was *Cotopaxi*. What other potential victims of the Bermuda Triangle might be hiding in plain sight?

Although we can speculate about what causes the Bermuda

Many believe the *Cyclops* lies at the bottom of the ocean like this wrecked ship.

DECLASSIFIED

Like other lost ships, the USS *Cyclops*'s disappearance wasn't noticed until she was days late to her destination. Maybe we would have more answers if the investigation had started sooner. This lack of evidence has led to many theories about *Cyclops*'s demise.

Some suggest that *Cyclops* was destroyed by an enemy U-boat, a German submarine. But Germany has no record of submarines in the area at that time. Others think that the German-born captain sabotaged the vessel in support of his homeland. Another theory is that a UFO plucked *Cyclops* from the sea.

The truth might be more boring. *Cyclops* was overloaded and had engine damage. A tropical storm was reported in the area at the time of her disappearance. Many people agree that these factors caused the ship to sink to a watery grave.

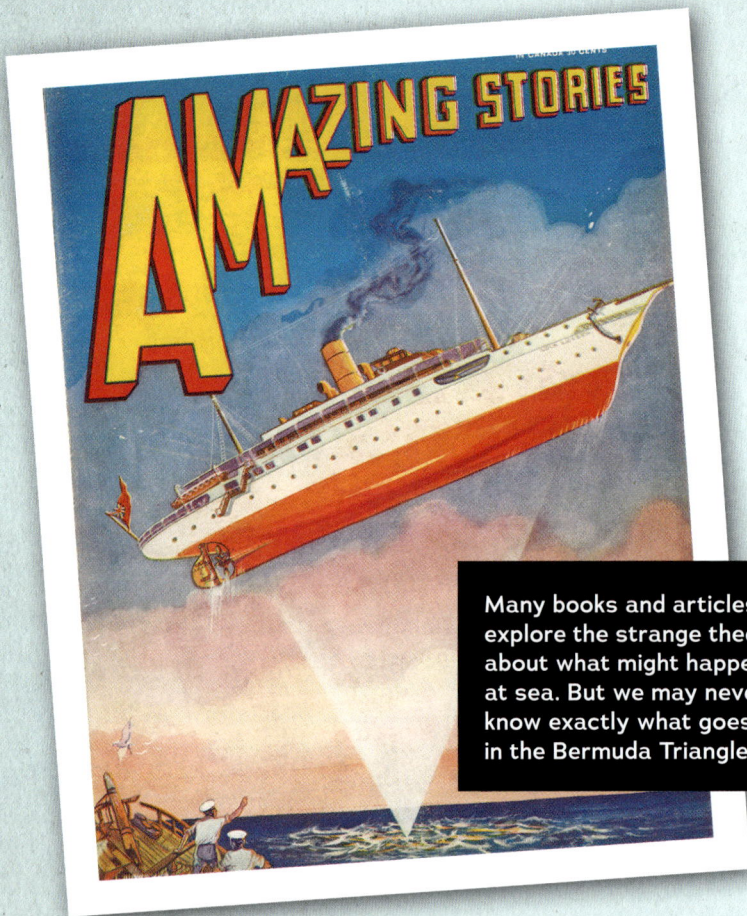

Many books and articles explore the strange theories about what might happen at sea. But we may never know exactly what goes on in the Bermuda Triangle.

Triangle disappearances, many questions remain. We will never know exactly what happened to ships and planes lost there without accounts from survivors. Perhaps *Cyclops* will be discovered lurking on the seafloor. Or maybe one day we will discover that we aren't alone in this universe after all.

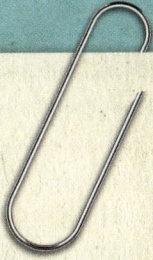

Timeline

1492: Christopher Columbus and his crew witness strange lights and their compass points off course.

1812: The *Patriot* sets sail with Theodosia Burr Alston on board and is never seen again.

1918: The USS *Cyclops* disappears after stopping in Barbados on the way to Baltimore, Maryland.

1921: The *Carroll A. Deering* is found abandoned on the coast of North Carolina.

1945: Flight 19 disappears on a training mission in the Bahamas. Then a rescue plane is also lost.

1949: The *Star Tiger*'s sister aircraft, *Star Ariel*, disappears between Bermuda and Jamaica.

1964: A magazine article coins the term "Bermuda Triangle" to describe a region of strange disappearances.

2020: A shipwreck discovered in the 1980s is confirmed to be the SS *Cotopaxi*, lost in 1925.

Glossary

anomaly: something that is different, strange, or not easy to classify

debris: the remains of something that has been broken down or destroyed

dimension: a way that things exist or are understood. For example, some people think time would pass in a different way in another dimension.

electromagnetic: something that is made magnetic by an electric force

extraterrestrial: space alien

phenomenon: something that happens, especially something remarkable

rogue: something that appears suddenly and is impossible to control

sabotage: to destroy or damage something on purpose

speculate: to guess or theorize

Learn More

Berne, Emma Carlson. *What Do We Know about Atlantis?* New York: Penguin Workshop, 2022.

Boutland, Craig. *Scary Alien Abductions*. Minneapolis: Lerner Publications, 2020.

Bowman, Chris. *Flight 19: Lost in the Bermuda Triangle*. Minneapolis: Bellwether Media, 2020.

Curious Kids: What Is the Bermuda Triangle and Why Is It Considered Dangerous? https://theconversation.com/curious-kids-what-is-the-bermuda-triangle-and-why-is-it-considered-dangerous-145616

Kids News: Solving the Mystery of the Bermuda Triangle https://www.kidsnews.com.au/explainers/solving-the-mystery-of-the-bermuda-triangle/news-story/f1139a5c6de8cacae249bc5895f62241

Mason, Jenny. *UFOs*. New York: Children's Press, 2022.

National Geographic Resource Library: Rogue Waves https://www.nationalgeographic.org/article/rogue-waves/

What Is Electromagnetism? https://mocomi.com/what-is-electromagnetism/

Index

Photo Acknowledgments

Image credits: yoshi0511/Shutterstock, p. 1; U.S. Department of Defense Archive/Alamy Stock Photo, p. 5; Tetra Images/Getty Images, p. 6; Gemini Pro Studio/Getty Images, p. 7; Classic Image/Alamy Stock Photo, p. 8; The Picture Art Collection/Alamy Stock Photo, p. 9; ShawshotsAlamy Stock Photo, p. 10; jovan vitanovski/Shutterstock, p. 11; furundul/Alamy Stock Photo, p. 12; MathieuRivrin/Getty Images, p. 13; ursatii/Getty Images, p. 14; Fer Gregory/Shutterstock, p. 15; FtLaudGirl/Getty Images, p. 16; Maryna Patzen/Getty Images, p. 17; Stephen Frink/Getty Images, p. 18; Posnov/Getty Images, p. 20; Denys Yelmanov/Shutterstock, p. 21; Extreme-Photographer/Getty Images, p. 22; Sally Newcomb/EyeEm/Getty Images, p. 23; ZUMA Press/Alamy Stock Photo, p. 24; john standing/Alamy Stock Photo, p. 25; Reinhard Dirscherl/Getty Images, p. 26; Chronicle/Alamy Stock Photo, p. 28.

Design elements: fotograzia/Getty Images; Ivan Gromov/Unsplash; Marjan Blan/Unsplash; Reddavebatcave/Shutterstock; AVS-Images/Shutterstock.

Cover: Victor Habbick Visions/Getty Images.